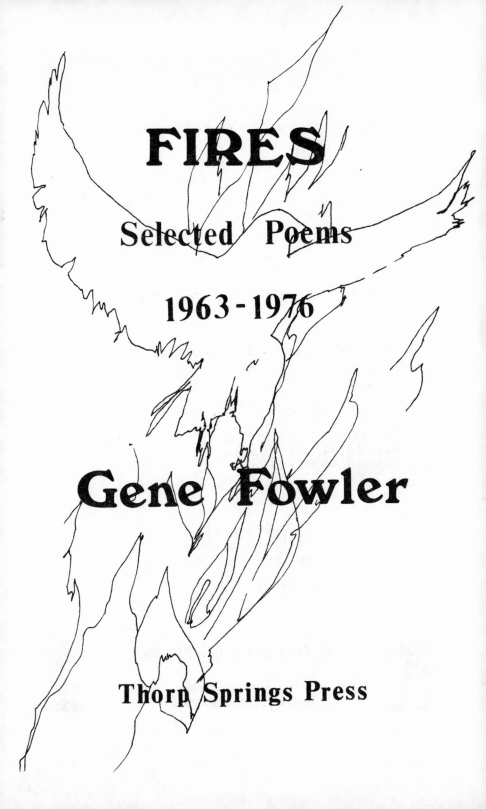

FIRES

Selected Poems

1963 - 1976

Gene Fowler

Thorp Springs Press

Cover and title page drawings by Amelia Gianelli

Library of Congress Cataloging in Publication Data

Fowler, Gene, 1931—
    Fires.

    Selected Poems 1963-1976
    I.   Title.
PS3556.083F5   1975   811'.5'4   75-19185
ISBN 0-914476-01-7 paper
ISBN 0-914476-51-3 cloth

THORP SPRINGS PRESS

23ll-C Woolsey Street
Berkeley, California 94705

AN INTRODUCTION

Since the early 1960's Gene Fowler's poems have been appearing regularly in the literary magazines. Six of his books have appeared from independent presses on the west coast: *Field Studies* and *Shaman Songs* from Dust Books; *Her Majesty's Ship* from Grande Ronde Press; *A Felon's Journal* from Second Coming Press; *Vivisection* and an earlier edition of *FIRES* from Thorp Springs Press. The largest samples of his work to appear from New York publishers are in *31 New American Poets* from Hill and Wang; and *The Smith Poets* from The Smith Press at 5 Beekman St., New York.

Wherever his poems appear they gear up interest and debate. His peers know Fowler is "making it new" in poetry; he is one of the few poets around who can *teach the ear,* a different order than merely improving our sensibility.

He has developed at least the first two elements of Ezra Pound's triune poetics *(logopoeia, phanopoeia, and melopeoia)* past the point where Pound left off. In the third realm, *melopoeia,* Fowler's rhythms, tied like Pound's to the Anglo-Saxon oarstrokes, and to the natural movements of the whole body—"the walking man"—are far more fruitful than, say, Charles Olson's "Projective Verse," which, with its trochees, has lapsed into the *school of tortured breathing.*

For an age which has hardly digested Ezra Pound, then, Fowler's poems will seem strange to many ears. This expanded edition of his selected poems, *Fires,* contains all of his long poems and the best of his shorter poems which have appeared since 1971, the date of the first edition. These long poems bear the mark of being so representative of our age they will surely outlast our age. Given the generally gray, quiet, confessional quality of most post World War II poetry, that alone is a singular victory, not just for poetry but for mankind.

Vivisection, the long poem detailing Fowler's five years in San Quentin prison (and I remind the reader that Ben Jonson had the mark of the felon branded in his palm) bears out his belief that this era's totem is "the caged beast." The United States is at least a match for the Soviet Union in the percentage of its people kept behind bars; in one society it's the *criminal mind* that's caged, in the other it's the *social deviant* or *parasite.* In all cases, in all climes, those who have been behind bars know the "Furies" that have been set upon us. In the past few years almost as many prison anthologies have appeared in the U.S. as there are prisons; none of this work, though much of it is fine, that has reached my eyes, seems to have the breadth and bite of *Vivisection.*

The positive response to the prison syndrome of our society (the office windows that never open; the claustrophobic security of even the mattress companies) is a deep return in the human mind to a consciousness of the earth and the human being's place on the earth as a *free beast,* lively walking the hills as the bear, the elk and the lion. The reawakening of the old ways of Native Americans, the awareness of their sense of the land, their sense of the tribe, and the life-bond between all that lives, has provided a profound and healthy shock to the consciousness of American society. There has been an enormous outburst of poetry, almost entirely in English, among Native Americans themselves. At the outset of this era, Fowler set down his *Shaman Songs,* as crystal clear today as when he wrote them a decade ago. This is ageless poetry, and poetry for an age.

All poets must survey their own era strictly in terms of what others are doing. As Pound does this in *Hugh Selwyn Mauberly,* so does Fowler in *Her Majesty's Ship.* Just as the reader must constantly be aware that Pound is writing in London for Londoners, so Fowler is writing in San Francisco for the west coast with its many pretentious "literary renaissances."

4

With regards to Fowler's other medium length poems, the reader might try reading aloud *The Seafarer* in an old man's voice. Much of Fowler's poetry has an oral quality which will only be touched when heard read aloud. The poem, *San Francisco*, and the counterpart poem for San Francisco's twin city, Berkeley, *Obsidian*, mark those points on the compass only as one who has walked all over these cityscapes at all hours of the day and night can mark them.

Many gems await the reader in this book of poems; not least of which is Fowler's overriding sense of *onomatopoeia*, that "deep pool of sounds" that permits mankind to speak the world, to make names. Fowler is a *name-maker* of the first rank. The Chinese concept which is congruent to this sense of language and sound ordering the poem, ordering experience, and linking "non-human phenomena and human law" is expressed in the word Lü*彳聿. Lü is law, music, number, and the regularity of the seasons. It is the sound and rhythms of the natural world, the movements of the heavens, that bring harmony into human life, teach our ear, and allow our speech. This Lü彳聿 is found in Gene Fowler's poetry.

—*Paul Foreman*

*Lu 彳聿, has as its right-hand phonetic 聿 a sign which was in most ancient times a hand holding a writing implement, and for its radical the word, 彳, which meant a step with the left foot, suggesting an original connection with the notation of a ritual dance, as that of a shaman's. See Joseph Needham's excellent discussion in Vol. II, *Science and Civilization in China.*

ACKNOWLEDGMENTS

This list of credits, missing from the first edition, was worked out over coffee in a sandwich shop by Paul Foreman and myself. There is an eleven year publishing history and I've not had the good fortune to live a life that permitted me to accumulate and keep an "ego file." It's all done with memories. Many poems have been reprinted many times—and I don't recall all those reprintings in magazines, books and anthologies. A few have been pirated, such as **The Words** by *Southern Review,* and **Shaman Song** 2 by *The East Village Other.* Here, then, is as complete a list as I can reconstruct. No publication or its editor or publisher is deliberately omitted.

—Gene Fowler

The Smith Poets; Freelance; Hyperion; Ante; Painted Bride Quarterly; Dust, San Francisco Chronicle; Illuminations; American Literary Anthology No. 1; Wood Ibis; Grande Ronde Review; Hanging Loose; 31 New American Poets; Avalanche; Mandalas; New, American and Canadian Poetry; Wild Dog; Synapse; Kayak; Towards a New America; Poetry Review; Amphora; Poetry Now; Obsidian; Out of Sight; and *Zahir.*
Many of these poems were also gathered in the books, *Field Studies,* and *Shaman Songs,* published by DUSTBOOKS; *Her Majesty's Ship* published by Grande Ronde; *A Felon's Journal* published by Second Coming; *Obsidian* as a broadside, *Vivisection* and an earlier edition of *FIRES* (1971) published by Thorp Springs Press.

TABLE OF CONTENTS

HER MAJESTY'S SHIP

VIVISECTION

INTRODUCTORY REMARKS

One handful of dirt at a time
My mountains slide into my valleys
Overloading the rock mantle.

Some hidden fault yields
Some deep part slides against another
And the outflying waves throw you back.

This is my flesh I speak.

VIVISECTION

for the human beings held
in San Quentin: 1954—9

PROLOGUE

> "You have sinned; such
> Furies as we know shall
> be set upon thee."
> — The Courts

Escape blossomed in the car
Freeway blood and me running down
Some endless, panting ditch; dreams
Die when the other end of the chain
Shrivels, snivels: God — me? Here?

The world singing, spinning, swooping
Through a point at the base of my skull:
To grey. To grey. Just four hours away.
Great stone grey.

Such
Furies as we know shall
be set upon thee.

I

Ah, half curl and skulk; seventy feet
Tall   the door closes against my back

Crack ! My back cracks, my soul swings
On hinges   behind my Death Mask

                    a pendulum
Penetrating the infinite steel
        the infinite steel   infinite steel

                    steel
                    lll; I am empty
My soul swings through infinite steel.
HELP ! I bend about my cracked spine
Echo under a vanished

                    ceiling.

Oh God, where are you? Damned, damned
. . . .

" Strip naked. Strip naked. Strip naked.
Strip . . . ." My legs are skinny; I am cold;
I am empty and naked; "What thin
Partitions" inside from outside divide?
Will I *implode* or *explode*? Why do you
Search my empty rectum with your Cosmic
Eye? You will see I am empty
And decide to collapse me, save a cell.
Hang me on your Warden's wall : an El Greco
Inmate. " Special exhibit here; came
to us from Hell, angry Hell." *Such*
            Furies as we know shall
                    be set upon thee.

II

No. Why can't it be a room?
Barred cave without even earth
Or water. Water. Water. Drowned.
In parched hope; I still press
My white chest against steel, flat
Infinite steel. Bulge, damn it; bulge
In just one spot : be a cave—
I'll carve a bison ; I'll color
It with pigments from eyes and bowels.
Let me *see*   somewhere *out.* Let me.
Let me

    see

     out.

My knee tastes salty. Shaggy beast
Remembering   being a man. Sham.

What peculiar affinity do I feel
For a soul swinging on infinite
Steel. Hinges. Was that nebulous
Food-stuff what made my *Now-It*

     a man thing?

    Such
Furies as we know shall
  be set upon thee.

III

The wind is so cold   blows
From all directions right now.

My fur
Just not thick enough today —
Cold   cold
cooooold.

If the therapists see my new fangs
They will call me *recidivist,* lock
Me at the other end of the hall
Past time; I must find and steal
A mask; I must look like a man thing.

The yard is so cold. So cold. I
Must find a mask with a red heart
On the forehead; every man thing
Has a red heart on its forehead.
The red heart bleeds.

Here the blood
Coagulates too fast; but therapists
laugh, nod knowingly, say "good."

The mask will cover my fur *(I must hide*
Shaggy beasts become recidivists.
My eyes are turning red; they burn
The surrounding skull;
My breath is hot.

Such
Furies as we know shall
be set upon thee.

IV

Dark. The cell is black dark
The tier lights gone with the storm.

The guards are teleologically afraid
Yellow bugs in the chaos. They

Would call for man things if they dared.
Guards have no hearts on their foreheads.

They are beasts. Not shaggy beasts
Like me. They whine; their eyes run

All over. They are hungry beasts
They hate man things   but lick them.

They bite my heels; I can't walk;
I slip in my blood, forget in the pain.

The lights are all out.
Escape!

I cry to be naked in the storm.

> *RAIN*
> run over my nose

> *MUD*
> caress my loins

> *run* to explode my legs

God, let me smell my soul   wet,
Clean from my fetid sweat, *Such*

*Furies as we know shall
     be set upon thee.*

V

Stone and steel many foetus womb
Honeycombe   we are " encased in infinite
Array." Listen to the beehive drone
Of us : Ha, we are a huge hum of hubris.
We buzz.

        Our sound swirls; then, one
Is loud against the other, one bee thing
          alone

A bee thing smashes his body
Against the blood washed edges of his cell

Thinking he is the daughter he smashed against
The dim wall of another cell   private   past.

        This time
He smashes himself against man's unyielding
   beeswax. He dies. Again. Again. Again.
        *

Music hour. The cacaphony of musical
Catharsis starts. The buzz is gone   replaced :
A mad myriad tongued voice makes a requiem

For the red and white thing carried off.

My stomach hurts. *Such
Furies as we know shall
    be set upon thee.*

VI

We sit in a long line
Beneath a frowning future that *hates*
Us. Inside is The Board.
They devour us one by one and spit
Out the chewed carcass that walks

16

Away with chunks
Gouged out of it.
They kill us each year; I have been
Killed twice before. Once last year
Once the year just before last year.
Each year they kill me a different way.
Maybe this year they will decide I
Have been killed enough times. Killed
Enough times.   *Such*
Furies as we know shall
       be set upon thee.

VII

Once I was a little boy
Who leaned against a tree and cried
Because I had to go to school.

The blanket is rough; the earphones
Just died.

              Stopped telling me
Man things are still in the world.

It is quiet and once I was a boy.
Once I was a man thing, too. Now
I listen to feet on the tier above.
The feet are counting us one by one.
A tiny window lies distant across a chasm.

In it lies a tiny moon
The moon I knew as a little boy *but*
grown small somehow   a model moon.

If they find it, they will collapse it
Hang it on the Warden's wall beside
An El Greco inmate. *Such*
   Furies as we know shall
        be set upon thee.

VIII

Domino players on the yard
Lined on the tables : wooden faces
With white and black eyes — players
And pieces alike without expression.

Rain comes; it is whipped around
The tables and under :

                              an angry wind
        A dervish mystically dancing pain.

Domino players on the yard
Don't see the rain; their ritual
Belongs to a God of the servo mechanism.

   My coat is thin, tugged about blue
   Ears. Click. Click. Click.
   Domino players on the yard
   Lined on the tables. *Such*
      Furies as we know shall
         be set upon thee.

IX

There never is another body
In my bed. Why can't the lovers
Of my fevered dreams be solid :
Solid enough to touch me in love?
I hurt
        with the rigid need.
All those inappropriate needs rise
Leap like ghosts to haunt my soul.

Is man after all a pre-set pattern
of responses

    robbed of meaning
When the glow of flesh comes? Emotion cries
Empty in the night. The dark is sexual.
But the lovers are all ghosts; they melt
In my fevered grasp and leave me cold:
"A black sheep with a crumpled horn."

     Such
Furies as we know shall
  be set upon thee.

X

Jute Mill. Jute Mill. Jute Mill.
4500 Voltaires burned the god damned Jute Mill.
Down. Down. Down. Down in the fiery dawn.

Oh ho! Authority has built a super steel
Monstrous. Stubborn. INFINITE Jute Mill.

It's fire proof. Love proof. Life proof.
IT EATS US. ITS EATS US. IT EATS US.

It eats us.   *Such*
Furies as we know shall
  be set upon thee.

XI

My knee tastes salty. Steel wall
Against my side tastes acid cold.

    Knee, buttock,
Shoulder, ear. Touch this shaggy beast.

We denizens darken and somehow dream:

I squat among my clothes
Before the fire; fire's tongues
Echo among the ruins; Night
Laughs; still I decode
Dead concepts, tracing formal
Symbols forever to know
A dead man. I see no sign
Of his world. Do not know him.

Morning light falls dead on the tier.
We stand to the bars — dream only of food.
Forgotten, the paleontological task and
Night fade and are lost; every morning
The task is lost.   *Such*
Furies as we know shall
be set upon thee.

XII

Have they killed me again? Or will I
Get my *time*? Finish your one by one count.

Have mail call
And give me my notice of *life* or *death*.

At the bars : I am a leper looking into a
mirror.

Will my evil show? Will the House of Lazarus
Disgorge me? Where is your dream Walt Whitman?

Will I taste in a week,
A month, a quarter   the sweet juices of your
Rich grasses?

Have mail call : give me my notice of *life* or *death*.

Please let me breathe. *Such*

Furies as we know shall
be set upon thee.

And you will wait
To know the sight of their faces.

Such
Furies as we know shall
be set upon thee.

XIII

Two months passed   one month more.
Two months since they told me what prize
I might lose in one minute. A hundred
And twenty nine thousand and six hundred
Minutes of *terror*. Now only forty three
Thousand and two hundred more to sweat.

Each drop of sweat plots its track
Leaving a livid snake scar where it runs.

I am criss crossed with down turning
Trails of acid sweat. *Such*
Furies as we know shall
be set upon thee.

XIV

Ah   I am beautiful

        today.

               What colors
In this new skin wrapped about my dead soul.

Today I go to heaven. Judgment is passed.
But I fear heaven more than I feared judgment.

        I AM AFRAID

My bladder runneth over almost. I will die
       when first I see that light.

I cannot live out there. I AM AFRAID.
I remember four years and nine months ago.
I remember Authority, its face bruised with guilt.

            "You have sinned; such
          Furies as we know shall
           be set upon thee."

STORM

for Tu Fu

Key fall.
And falling leave
                glyphs
black on white
vanish in the slip stream
across white shoals.
Under heated blood
                fingers
caress keys
into fall.
Storm clouds pile up
off the coast.
Tea kettle
                dries
splits
hisses.
Old metal in Hellfire.
Echo wind coming up.
Black sun
under the ribs broods
the uselessness of letters.

A DAY AT THE BEACH

i   *Morning*

killer whales
frisk like dolphins
a freighter
marks the horizon
rifle gallery cutout
   come to life
of a crisp morning

      sand pipers
  chase waves
back into the sea
cloud waves ride winds
  inland
lungs fill with salt
chew meat out of it

      feet sink
in dry sand
  cut cookies shaped
like feet
in wet sand

     kick up
abandoned shells
   in sand

the long sea rises
  from night green waves
like aphrodite

ii   *Playing Catch*

i find pebbles
  in the wet sand
dark agates
veined in white

24

dull bloodstones
    blue green bits
of fossilized sea
smoothed glass
   taken from men
returned as pebbles
i grind my knee
   in the sand
a rough wearing
a sound of the sea
   an erosion
scrape knuckles
taking up pebbles
   the sea has left
i run heavily
   in the tight sand
kicking up foam
throwing the pebbles
   far out
to sea and waiting
for them to wash in

iii   *Evening*

   the sea shatters
around the rocks
white and green sparks

nature's cutting torch

     tears swell
roll down tight cheeks
mix with the salt spray
   on my lips
burn the tip of my lick
ing tongue

i wonder why i'm crying

25

THE SEAFARER

Hang it all, Ezra Pound
there can be but one "Seafarer."
But Seafarer, and my Seafarer?

Allow,   a tired man th' tellin
a all he's got, th' hurt an th' past.
Th' storms an' damages? Those I'll tell
ain't like none yew'v bin told.
It's brine soakt bread, an' moldy,
was all t' eat, an' th' old hull
can't count th' angry seas
hev beat its boards, bent its sail;
an' I'v stood alone, near topside down,
close enuf cliffs I cud touch 'em, feart
m' drownin, an' God allus meant for men
t' stay aground an' suck th' soil.
Fearin t' drown an' m' feet near froze.
Th' night wind 'd come up cold,
make a man's eyes int' ice.
I'd look int' th' sea, stare in th' sea.
I'd see faces a uncles an' cousins
an' fancy I saw th' face a m' sweetie.
An' th' faces 'd break, split an' grin,
th' laughin of a albatross in th' water.
Ice on m' hands an' m' eyelashes.
Th' whole winter, haunts wooin
me, gamin me in m' grog.
Storms, on th' hard bord we followt;
off th' cliffs, ice feathers
fell on th' stern; th' eagles 'd scream
spray wingd.

Not any knowin
'r havin 'll make a man happy
if th' sea-smell sucks his head.

It seems mad t' th' solid settlt
with makin money an drinkin wine.
A night comes, snow from th' north,
an' cold ground comes thru m' boots.
Th' ground is too hard t' dig again.
Th' howlin an' bumpin in a late bar
ain't nothin t' a star on a clear night
pointin a way a man kin go.
I git a edge, go all restless.
They laugh an' gloat; I hunt a ship.
A man with hair in his ass won't stay
his life one place from born t' dies.
There's a whole world t' win
for a man with brain an' muscle an' eye.
Given any here, there's more,
much more, t' be had with a turn a sail.
Th' winner, th' rich, th' well-wed:
each has a wish he'd bin t' sea.
Holdin m' sweetie, I see a star
along her shoulder, white past white;
an' nothin but salt, water n air,
not beauty a woman nor beauty a land,
will hold m' head, will hold m' heart.
Th' lumps in th' bar smell no sea,
hear no waves grindin a hull.
There's a world burstin m' head
an' they'll never know it's there.
I'll go as whales go.
I'll suck ocean an' spit foam
an' be a eagle, fly away.
What'll I save, stayin sheltert?
Th' life is loand an' men on land
spit a lung or wrinkle t' death
or curse it away in blood n bile
on a knife's dirty edged suck.

Ain't no man lived always.
An' every big man eggs
on those who live t' say his name,
t' sing his lauds, t' lie his death
away with tales a deeds he done,
Revel in deeds.
                            Dry rotted
days an' who cares what's won?
Th' winnin ain't what it was.
Th' big spenders hev baggd th' spoils.
Wha'ever's bin won is all a joke.
There's nothin to it.
Men die, th' world stays.
Women 'r riches? Worries rest.
Th' grave is quiet, th' blade rustet.
A man gits old, his blood gits thin.
They'r gone. All gone.
Th' best I'v known 'r buried bones.
Nary a one got a woman,
moves a hand, makes a dream,
feels any quiver left a hope.
If he poundet coffins out from gold
he'll find bones th' only hoard.

WINTER LIGHT

       Thick
         hawk winged
cloud bar
sliding across the Pacific,
dark swallower
filling the whole view,
sweating
hungry for the land.
Water hissing
          in the rocks,
grey breath licking me.
Water
      green foil crinkling
      dirty white scuffles
      ruffling and panting.

Salt on my face
draws flesh into a jerkied tough sheet
burying me
       in crystal
grey light

       frozen
       onto my skin.

SHAMAN SONGS

Hunting Song

a preface

When the moon
stays into morning
when the river
calls loudest the dawn
it is our time to hunt
And we hunt
the first bear

*Speak Shaman   How do we find
the bear*

With the coming of night
build a fire
that you may see my words
With the coming of night
dance by the fire
that you may feel my words

*We see Shaman   We see
your words
by the fire
We dance Shaman   We feel*

your words
by the fire.

Your bodies grow large
My words are flesh
on your limbs
We dance the flesh

Your skins grow shaggy
My words are fur
against the cold
We dance the fur

Your scent grows keen
My words are winds
with their secrets
We dance the scent

You run on fours
Run true on fours
My words are bears
with their secrets
We dance the bear
We dance the bear

Now you know the bear
We dance the bear

You know his ancestors
We dance the bear

You know his trails
We dance the bear

When the moon
stays into morning
you will catch the bear

1

My ancestors were shamans.
But i am not my ancestors.
I am shaman
to a tribe recently come.
A tribe with gas turbines.
A tribe with horror of Being
    homosexual.
A tribe with a bomb.
A tribe with fear of the Other.
    Foreign man.
    Black man.
    Sexed man.
    High man.
    Other.
A tribe with fear of the Other.
I wear animal skins
and cast huge shadows on the wall
And the old men sit in council,
sit at their fire.
They wonder
if i am their shaman.
Or if i am the Other.

2

on taking a coal from the fire
in naked fingers

The word
is in the hand.
Under the moon
in the hand.
At the head of the valley
in the hand.
It glows in the hand.
Here!

Look here
in the hand.
Look at the word
in the hand.
It glows.
A great translucence
in the hand.
Go thru the translucence
in the hand.
Into the world
in the hand.
The coals glow
in my fire.
Are words
for the hand.

3

You calld me, always, to heal you
when sickness came to you.

You calld me, always, to read you
the best path for the hunt.

>Now you build
>your fires big

>but your skins
>are not warm

>Now your pots
>are empty

>but you seek
>no new game.

You calld me, always, to help you
and my magic was strong.

You calld me, always, to help you
when trouble came to you.

Then you said
my gods ate

what you could
not yet spare.

Then my songs
made you stand

where the storm
might come out.

You calld me, no more, to heal you
when sickness came to you.

You calld me, no more, to read you
the best path for the hunt.

Near my tent, you drop your head.
At my fire, your smile is stiff.
Still, you do not call.

4

I will journey
to a place where i may see
what each day we see.
These old friends will be
shaped and colord fires.
Heat and light will burn
within my eye.

I will journey
to a place where i may see
what we do not ever see.
I will write names in my blood.
When heard, the names will burn
within your eye.

34

I will journey
to a place where i may see
that which there is to see.
There, your eye and mine
will become a single eye.
That which i see will burn
as our eye.

5

I have journeyd.
I return with scarrd flesh.
I return with tattoos burnd
in my meat.

I have journeyd.
Now i sit at my tribal fire.

I sit and watch tattoos dance
on my skin.

I have journeyd.
Now i let you watch my flesh.
I let you watch stories unfold
on my surface.

I have journeyd.
Now i try to relate my stories.
You are lost in dancing images
on my corpse.

I have journeyd.
Let me return.

6

I have shown you
coals in the fire.

Words in the soul.

Look at one coal,
a single coal taken

up into my fingers,
safely in the flesh.

Look
deeply into the coal
til the eyes sting
til the eyes cry out.

Move closer to the coal.
The flame does not flare
but it has not coold.
It has grown in heat.

See
the deep rooted fires.
See
the dark private places.

Move down into the coal.
Feel the flesh as flame.

Where is this place?
What are the names?

Who are the shapes
moving about you?

Who the live dark spots,
the living white flame?

Whose flesh is flame?
Where is your eye?

7

It is the woman who grows things.
He who would make the rain fall
must be as the woman.

The body must be cut and turnd.
The dark and moist soil of night
brought to the sun.

He who would make the rain fall
must walk unclothd in the night
must be as the woman.

Hold the seed in careful fingers.
Seed that comes from every field
with its songs told.

Seed that comes from every field
must be planted in the bright sun
and left in the night.

The seeded and moist soil of night
will call and join the sun and rain.
The moon will feed you.

8

The eye is clear with the dawn.
The nostrils are wide in the wind.
The legs are strong from their sleep.
The arms that reach for the sun
    reach far over mountains.

    Run fast as the deer.
    Taste the wind as the rabbit.
    Be strong as the bear.
    See with the eagle's glint.
    Hear as the lynx hears.

The known trails are dry and fast.
The new trails are wet for tracks.
The game is unrested, out and moving.
The legs that reach for the sun
    reach far over mountains.

Trail as the jackal.
Change rivers as the beaver.
Strike slyly as the weasel.
Strike fast as the rattler.
Steal as the crow steals.

Bring our tribe the needed meat
sighting the cooking fires from far
the night growing behind you.

9

four invocations to fish

i

Night's wing hides the sun.

O, dark fish run fast
thru cold streams and rivers
that prowl in raven's house.

Dance in white waters.
Become many in black waters.

Become many and dance.

I will carry stones and earth
to mouths of rivers and streams
make deltas, make shallow places.

If the waters are made shallow
the fish must run near my hand.

O, dark fish run hard
into my quick hand.

ii

Night's wing falls
opens a thunder of sunlight.

O, bright fish run fast
thru spotted streams and rivers
that walk in long grasses.

Dance in light waters.
Become many in dark waters.

Become many and dance.

I will wade into the waters
til the two parts of my body
walk side by side.
I will catch the fish
if he does not know where i am.

O, bright fish run hard
into my quick hand.

iii

The raven and the golden hawk
have swallowed one another.

The birds of the sky are gone.
They took the sky with them.

I walk where day and night
do not embrace as lovers.

Many shades of day follow
and there is no beginning
and there is no end.

I wake and it is not light.
I sleep and it is not dark.

My only hope to find the day
my only hope to find the night

is to fish ghost waters, to fish
ghost waters for the coal fish.

    I must fish with a dance.
    I must fish with a song.
    I fish for the night.
    I fish for the day.

    O, coal fish come burn
    with light and dark places.

    O, coal fish hurry now
    into my quick hand.

    I will reach into your
    fiery heart, pull out
    the sky

iv

I hide the day in one hand.
I hide the night in one hand.

I fish in eight directions.
I fish among the many suns.

The fish i hunt will run
the spotted sky

dance away in light waters
we call stars

become many in dark waters
we call distances.

All forms are his form.

    O, terrible fish run hard
    into my quick hand.

    And your fire and dark
    will be my flesh.

40

10

each man's lust is a cult

The rains are warm.
Our valleys and plains are almost green
               —under blades of grass so slight
                a blade is seen only by a keen eye
from the height of a walking man.

The strong women who have born sons are restless.
The ripe girls who have come thru the winter
   watch the sun walk across the day.
Their eyes gentle as the wind, tender as the new grass.

The shaman's tent is prepared for fire and dances.
The ripe girls who have come thru the winter
   watch the sun go away across the day.
The men look at the girls' throats and breasts in wonder.

              Night lands, breathes
its strange winds around our closed tents, and fires
   breathe their forms onto the circling hides.

    Women must be torn from girls in a cruel stench
of dance filld flesh and full thighs.

       On stetcht hides of the shaman's tent
woman Gods mimic the first wild dances
             —thundercloud dancers in a sacrament.

Stolen tusk of a grandfather buffalo.
Unfalling carvd phallus of our tribe.
My corded arm is painted to the elbow
in the red rains of our Spring.

The sudden women shine at the river, trickt
   from winter with a dance's thundercloud rise.

   The rains are warm, our valleys and plains green.

11

O, thunder cloud
        buffalo robe
of the sun—
how can you warm the sun?

                The woman's belly
                        swells, summer melon
                ready to split.
                It warms my fingers

        Dreamer's eye
                a magic star, grows
        in one night
        to twice its old size.

Thru the grey cloud
        lies a hidden sun
roasting potato—
no one to eat its warmth.

O, thunder cloud
        roasting robe
of the sun—
i will rip you open.

12

We have made hawks
that fly
where no hawks have flown.

We have made hard sky
and look out at the rain.

We have made warm hides
from no animal yet slain.

42

We have made horses
that stride
as no horses ever known.

    But, we are weak.
    On our wounded plains, we are alone.

We have forgotten
the shape and cry of our bellies.

We have forgotten
the dances of our own faces,
the songs of our own voices.

We have forgotten
the chants of the souls
in our running feet.

    Now, we remember.
    In our weeping tents, we are alone.

13

    shaman stands on the pre-dawn
    mountain, a dark mane on a thundercloud

i

One by one, all the old men of the tribe die, one
    by one, all the old women, all the young men,
all the young women,
even our children—
They all die.
The crows steal our eyes and fly beyond mountains.

The people of our tribe curl in trees, take on
    the color of the desert, and the desert begins
to swallow our plains, to pull down our mountains,
    to burn our winds into blackend breaths.

Our skin and bones grow old as the desert, become
  rock of the desert.
Where our eyes lookt out, there are now dark caves
  in twisted desert trees.

> *Ha he ye ya he ha-a-aa*
> I walk among the trees.

> *Ha he ye ya he ha-a-aa*
> Faces are gone with ghosts.

> *Ha he ye ya he ha-a-aa*
> I bury them in trees.

> *Ha he ye ya he ha-a-aa*
> Sorrow shakes my knees.
> I, too, find my tree.

> *Ha he ye ya ha-a-aa*
> *Ha he ye ya he ha-a-aaa*

When the dawn fire rises, where will we be?

ii

You few, who have listend, must rise
and leave the tree.

You few, who have heard, must gather
your magic and go.

> I cannot tell you
> what you take with you

> but, it burns, a coal
> planted in your center.

> I cannot tell you
> the magic names you know

> but, they wait, alive
> planted in your center.

You few, who have listend, have known
my magic was strong.

You few, who have heard, will know
your magic is strong.

> You have seen my gods
> and given them more

> than you had to spare.
> You must grow your gods.

> Skin and bones must become
> rock, the ghost must rise

> and fill you and burn.
> You must grow your gods.

You few, who have listend, have calld
my magic and eaten.

You few, who have heard, must call
your magic and grow.

Near my tent, you lift your throat.
At my fire, your smile beckons.
Still, you must not call.

iii

When those who left the trees
              have no more magic

when the ghosts who left
              are in ghost trees

stronger shamans than i, shamans whose
              eyes burn as suns in the sky
                  shamans whose
              eyes burn as stars in the night

will come.

Their magic will stand on the shoulders
               of my magic, my strong magic.

Their magic will ride on my magic
               as a tall warrior rides, standing
               on the shoulders of a great stallion.

And brushing the ghost trees with fingers warm as suns

          those ghost shamans
will make the ghosts to walk
     again in great tribes.

MORNING SONG

folding up my legs
bringing everything closer
to the surface
getting ready to dump
my mind into the lake
prophets are chemists
all the solids must go
into suspension
invite rearrangement
this dance sitting still
the mystic's wonder
seems inhuman
fire-man squatted down
on nickle steel asteroid
dreaming tiny galaxies
this account
a cold white light
flesh to be added
the bone and meat
waiting
knees rubbed sore
and cold
pressed into dew wet
grass
hands blue white
in a cold morning lake
reaching slow motion
for a fish
teeth chattering
early wind running sparks
across my skin
highland lake cut clean
as blue emeralds
raw green sea piling up

white capped rust rivers
of nitric acid on Mars
always the same
mirror
the dance
tears returning
placental fluids
the universal solvent
high plateau sun
tearing apart the atmosphere

XANADU

        i
        turn on
        with just
        poems
                (Primer)

Ancient oriental peace pipe
and tar baby.
King Kong on the skyline—
Solomon's eye
burning out the forehead.
Dreaming ape
following an underground river,
following it out
to cloud-banked sea.
Scenting agriculture:

loose black dirt
running ten miles,
trees full blossom
            drawing bees,
and old trees
been there forever
And down one slope
a broken place split back
            rocky cunt
bending the air.
(shade woman crooning
            under some far moon
            for a shaggy lover)
Out of split rock
blue geyser
climbing the air,
dropping back
coming again
water panting
and broken chunks of rock
                riding it
dancing rocks
and wild cat-
aract.

Five miles outland the river
                snaked,
headed
for the flat oiled sea.
Down through crevices.
Under the oiled top water.
                And in it—

voices
of apes (looked around and withered
and gone)
howling *war!*

49

Shadow pushing at tear-winged fog
and coming in low
a tight packed sun patch;
in it the beat
from the geyser and caves:
Sun yellow and blue ice shot through.
Black girl. Black girl.
Spiral belly button.
Playing guitar blue fingers
singing a mountain.
King Kong grunting
"trying to remember" hum—
if i could pull back that tune
catch hold
wind it into a solid line
and weave a sunny patch.
Sweat loose. Suck ice.
Apes coming to look and shout.
"Look out! Look out!"
"His eye's on fire!"
"His hair is spikes!"
"Better walk on around him."
"And keep your eyes shut."
"He's smokin'."

Hey!
Shit
gotta go see
my Avon lady.

SAN FRANCISCO POEM

only city i know
where you walk over a mountain
        on sidewalks, past bars
with beer smell and men laughing
                not a sign of the top
just night and fog
smell of wet wool as overcoats go by
                walk up til thighs
are bunched tight, walk down
til knees wobble, or
just lie down and roll to Market

belly dancing fog
        builds and hides half-seen women
to feed the thirst
coiled and rattling in my dream
dark spies to skulk and fear at edges
        of my shooting range
while i swell into a blazing sun of dream

                night fog gliding inland
on naked, sexy feet
here's the city you'd love to fuck

every poet i know
has a poem, somewhere, shivered out
        of rain-marshed parks and cobblestones
and brick water tanks against the next
        holocaust
about the Siren who hoots thru raukus horns
        at night from far away in the night
the ghost woman
whose orgasm rattle sounds like cable cars
                flower vendors and tongues
from all the continents

51

i keep feeling her finger tips
ice wet with night fog and hunger for her
working down thru my legs, dancing
my feet
in some comic jig
beads of mist
cosmic rosaries, sequences mazed over
forgotten sand dunes
                              old Italians liking
the sound
of their dialect, even late at night, the smell
        of red wine and pasta and sweaty work clothes
home ainta dead
if you'ra still eata it
and i knew a North Beach painter put Naples Yellow
on his tongue

to see, Jesus —it tastes like paint

ten years ago
sitting late in a coffee house
writing poems in long shadows and flickered yellow
        from a hoarded candle
was the short way home, the mystic streetcar
and the poets were heroes in Holy Book novels, now
it's all dead

                    walking out late at night
kicking bits of newspaper
walking past silent Negroes on doorstoops, who look
out of dark eyes
where the wind stops
the new poem, coffee smeared, in my fieldjacket pocket

i wonder how to tell the keepers
of fashion

the value
of a table whose evening rent is one cup of coffee
and my friends are always
moving

Chinatown garbage
lining the sidewalks, in tins and crates mysteriously
marked out from our East, off, somewhere, to the west
*   sharp fish and seaweed and poultry smells*
the sea
drug up on land by strong backs
and knowing bellies, under the eyes
of uncountable years

my city taking on an ivory tint, her eyes
going soft
as aged silt in the paddies where food grows

*   i squat down and rock*
between my feet
until the strain in my back is a long history
run my fingers over the rough
*   grey grain*
poke at a rubbery bit of food
i don't need
*   and the dawn comes*

*   the topless pens*
are being cleaned out
under the cool midmorning sun
*   somewhere the girls*
sleep, breasts wrapped in blankets
moist thighs tucked up under that dim
oder of the sea

she's cool in her morning frock, but i've known
    her on hot, rumpled mornings, after the bad
nights

up over hills, around the corners of buildings
across the brick water storage tanks
past iron gated stores
National Guardsmen spent a night sitting
or walking
reminding dark and frightened men and women
this town is someone else's whore

wonder who gets her
been all over her
like a kid petting, never getting
IN

but she's too mellow
for a virgin

ocean rolling in
big cement wall scraping my ass thru my pants
sky a pale blue cavern
distant

as an alien cathedral

once a guy told me go to church to meet girls

wonder
will i maybe meet San Francisco
here

ECOLOGY

a rain ends
in last splattering drops,
trees rough
and dripping
rammed into thick
tart smelling grass
shoes squish.

Air, full of water, smells
heavy, smells of
grasses, of sap
from broken limbs, of
fishes washed out of ponds.

My legs grow ancient
and I need to rest;
I am full of heaviness,
press down into my soles
and through them.

A bench is wet against me, then
steaming
at my weighted touch,
pushing up; the sky
comes down
breaking at my skin's million
closed mouths,
pressing gently, steadily
down.

I breathe in
a sky!

I feel it thick within
and my skin tingles open.

I breathe in
           a whole sky.

I yawn a sun.
The trees begin to dry; I watch
them drying
to matte in yellowed light,
my own rough chiseled bark
warming into breath.

IN THE GARDEN OF MY LADY

> long walks
> talking to invisible virgins
> —from LARVAE V

i

a woman partly known

ivory, skin like ivory, the poets
have spoken of that, cliched the awareness

but ivory is not a carved figurine
ivory is a rush thru jungle, a terrible cry

you walk naked
thru the room, all the times
i've taken you, undone

the whole act to do again, not
a ritual, but a true first coming

recurrence, all the memory
taken out with the new promise

the lust, a heat in my fingers
an expanding of the breath in my

belly, and you are only walking
across the room, my need the nakedness

we have

the muse
chased thru crowded streets, watched
furtively on streetcars and in restaurants
isn't some enigmatic featured goddess
but more often a young girl
just aware of her body, and full
of laughter

i bite your side
just above the pelvis, where the body turns
i want   more

what hunger dreams of tearing into flesh
what impossible lust do i growl out of
where is the strangling secret of possession

the hands
that claw at your breasts
aren't even my own hands

your cry of pained joy, your most
honest moment is my solitary lie
taken from you in my terrified quest for the dream

i run my tongue to the salt and acid taste
the vulnerability and count the cries
claw at tender breasts to rip out the cries

*thighs at the sides of my throat, raised
to my temples, known suddenly so intimately, and
the impossibly different thighs seen on beaches
in magazines   in other beds*

*what is this need, stroking your body, for other
bodies, what is this need, with perfection, for other
perfections*
why, running my tongue
over those other strange lips that never
become familiar, do i weep

why, when my body swells to speak of its health
and i raise myself across your body, stretching
and crushing your soft shapable breasts
under my hard ribs, thrusting
my flesh into your flesh, feeling the warmth
like a hand, even to its fingers that grab

and caress   and dance with you, batter
the muscles into joy with the forced reaching

why, then, does my throat twist with the sense
of something departed just as i arrived

i fall asleep
my mouth upon your breast
and dream of other women

                    ii.
                         the knowing of a woman
                                        (for hilary)

cold sea water rides onto the sand
washes foam around your folded knees

laughter, the delight, rises and sails
out over green water and floating things

fingers reach to trap the water
and it twists and ducks past them, cool

and inevitable as the flow of time

free in the sky
where land and sea touch

your body turns
slight as a boy's, fertile
as far inland soil, breasts
so my belly burns

a sea gull rides
the gentle after wave crest

i touch as lightly
as i can your water dried skin

trace the navel
and a line of the bottom rib

        the sea comes up, drops and slides
                  into foam
        a woman's cleaved flesh, a man's home

no words follow my gentle finger
dumb, i wish i might already have spoken
that your cheek might lift, turn the light
your eyes rise to mine with an answer

the gulls pull easily away from the water
their shadows race thru long sequences of shapes
                           the sea sings softly
sings softly in a dusk come into a dawn

i reach past your down turned eyes
my eyes blind as on the first day of sight
and loosen the halter of your swim suit

        the long beach lies naked in red light
                 curved and swollen
        your flesh comes to me as something stolen

    and i am running in mud foamed water
        the sun a hot burn on my shoulder

             as i

pull the last wet clothe away from you
trace the length
of your gentle movements, so lightly

60

my fingers feel you thru some molecule
    of air

                  your closed eyes soft mounds

    in the red light

echoed, then, in the breasts that ride your breath
as the sea rides its waves

                      diamonds of water

          tiny yellow sapphires of sand

crushed out of sight
as i lay my cheek on your belly

                how easily my body fits to yours
                      comes to yours
                the sea rides under us, seeking its
                      ancient shores

my hands, my arms   circle your head
draw it hard into my chest, my legs urging
yours back, away
and our bodies ride with the sea

        the sea's rising goes on   and breaks

            men would say it is then i have known you

we pull back, apart
your gripped brows move apart, soften
and the half-smile at your lips is drawn back
    into you

your opening eyes meet mine, and

              i know you

iii.

the discovery of a woman

(for jacquie)

redwood kings
pine queens, herding smaller breeds
and saplings in a wind stroked orgy
of westward travel over the vulval lips of our coastlands

> *it's all a birthing and the torrential nights*
> > *when speech left and spitting singing breakers*
> > *ran over the land*

> *coastlines forgotten in merging seas*
> *and a preparation was undertaken*
> > *for these dancing trees*
> *and their dances*

quiet people sititng in a room quietly
fire warmth and visiting
light

these several people
eyes and lower lids in shadow
devil smiles tossed in
to those eyes by old logs that cackle
and snort at these oft tossed
smiles the smilers never see
and the pretty copper haired girl
on the floor by the fire
listens

dark brows entwined and tense over
green eyes serious
as opals in a temple
poets reading

from burnt umber parchments, scraping
dust away from words poorly remembered
and ancient
cracked shadows hover about the fire
as their tales are retold or mistold
ghost image throats bent and swollen
the heat
of wanting to talk

eyes flame with sparks of blue, red, yellow
molecules
in a young, pulsing brain move
over
gentle flesh is changed
under thin, hiding clothe

among the trees a house
imago mundi
        a singular place of ritual where the initiates
go, most to fail

go   sit   wait
leave wondering at the rustling leaves
in their bellies
when the fall night of the ghosts is done
the night when failed initiates broke vigil
                fell asleep in the house, not knowing
it was a ceremonial house
and ghosts returned to the fire, dying in its embers
with whistled moans and explosive tubercular coughs

i'm going to get a nap
downstairs
and when it's time to go to the city
come wake me
i'll drive everybody to the city

in the room's center
    (ignorant of the girl's departure)
emptied red mountain wine bottles wedged together
a center post
rising to the ceiling, beyond
the ceiling the sky of which the poems spoke
dark with a silver ball of light
rolling its arc

the tales continue, the tellers
yawning, rolling
into blankets, deciding to stay
the city to wait
soon enough the city next afternoon
fire drawing in
a tiny red cluster

                    i'll tell jacquie to go to sleep
                    we don't need
                    a ride to the city

the floors, separate houses
and the outside dark, descending
overgrown hillsides

the girl asleep
her whole body darkened in black clothes
slacks and sweater
a dark corner of the night wrapped around
her
the fire of her hair
gone dark
the vigil above broken
sleep
the wrapping night to be torn away

the touched shoulder turns
brown eyes
are thickets, the dark woods where death
is undiscovered
and gentle furred things run safely
without eyes

> *you came, she said later, and that*
> *she had known me for a very long time, and had waited*
> *for the time when i would know her*

> *in a ceremonial house*
> *not break the vigil or forget the rituals*
> *not climb the center post for the easy sky*
> *but come into the beginning*

> *pull the real sky*
> *from where it is coiled in azure strands of lacy*
> *delicacy*
> *in the violet embers of her center*

when we rose
she had told me the mysteries
promised
     i am strong   and not greedy

the sun
drew greens out from the window framed trees

a magician
discovering similar but unique
rabbits

three
we go, now, to circle the mountain
walking where none has walked
a path, neat wooden steps, cut back bushes
a wooden bridge
none used, fresh cut lumber, all the greens
searing our nostrils

Afternoon late, fall, earlier overcast
pulled back
and coming on time for a sun cut
by a rearing horizon

no sunset here
sun flashes, sun flooding, sun
pulses
a lessening, a loss of color
the horizon coming in

in slow motion
a series of paintings so hard

brushes are ripped from our hands
our hands
smashed, crippled, made claws
to hold, as stands hold, what we are given
the man :
what a lovely place to make love
the woman :
oh yes
my agony :
what of those who would come and step over you

the wind against a cheek
my cheek
eyes a cold burn and vision
coming bleak and hard as an enemy

iv.

woman on the mountain

(for roger & joan)

we ascended in a car
a sunday afternoon, a way of tourists

filled with lusts, able to look only habit ridden
going where none has gone
seeming only to follow a hard trampled path

the driver
filled with war, hearing his waiting war
sick with the dark of it
i watch his eyes walking out over the land

see his hands on the wheel curl more gently
to hold earth, trees, sky, the Earth

he's trying to duck the push of time, trying
to fasten his soul to this place
and time

my hand on his shoulder, his reaching
to touch
i pull my hand back like a thief
the woman's hand easily on his other shoulder
a dark man in the far corner
i reach foreward again
he'll go to his waiting war, my hand
will remain, safe

the hills and woods and sky stay out of it

we all look at their greater beauty
and call it reasons
the dark man joined others, we left him
for a little while

the man, the woman
holding hands
i hold the woman's hand, the path
holding our circle open

another is here, of course, dark flesh ungathered
her song here, telling me
she comes
not for my eye, yet, more a scent
sap of a broken limb
the man, the woman

they know she is here, they are lovers
know my lover is here

she holds back, stays intangible, leaves
me a third, and weeps
for these lovers
for God's sake, pull me out, leave
them alone

she is gone

three
on an outcropping of rock, standing like Gods
lights coming on below us and above, the sun pulling out
the man : *don't move!* scrambling back
the woman and i left standing
wonder, the woman, all orange reds and whites
oh oirish lass
the man, shy of the woman
speaking of my beard against the sun and sky

his mind is a camera, today, because the anguish
of being a mind would kill him

it is night and we walk to the circle and on
across the little bridge

speaking of other places, looking
furtively at the mixed night and sun

we will drive down the hill

where are these two people
just now
where that other woman
who touched my cheek

         v.

             women wearing flesh

                          (for Marcia Danuser Singeman's
                          Company of young dancers)

divine union
a mystic wedding lost in the black clouds
of the past, the first
wedding, the poet and the dancer

tribute paid, again, by every poet, garlands set into
his titles, the movement and dreams of his poems
the marriage of poet and dancer

the poem that strays from music, the music that strays from dance
lost, said Ezra
the poet stretching and turning, in astral being
reaching to the dance with tenuous arm, ghost stuff, the flesh
left still and ugly, humped over desk, legs flaccid while the star being
leaps and turns in the bright dust of God's eye

                      and the dancer, the flesh dancer, caught
                      in gauze, echoing skin, echoing muscles, turning
                      glass eyes on the poet, eyes ranging back in time
                      choreographed, frozen to the spinning web, set
                      unseeing against the pulsing lungs ranged in the
                      dark pool before the stage

69

oblivion, dark auditorium
full of breath and waiting, temper pulled tight
muscles set, centered at the point of breath   on stage
auras of half color, set on dust
nubile dancers
eyes focused on patterns invisible
                              breath waiting

black box, *kosmos*
taut figures of fertility
breast pulled taut, crotch encompassing

candlepower subordinated, all echoed
in my moving intestines
centuries of common law, career dreams
pattern hypnosis   inpenetrable wall, infinite hymen

Organ of Pereeption, Hall of Light
set into community
the Third Eye, triangulation point, taken from the secret skull
projected for group Eros
hinted dark triangles at the fluid crossroads of flesh
set into moving arrangement, never still for grasping, *kosmos*

the breaths, polyrhythmic, set in darkness
growing grey and feeble, aged by ungraspable movement
sinking back into hollow locations, the Seats of souls, of breath
points in darkness, stopping, dying, reborn, polyrhythmic
pillars of salt marble rising, darkness   black Goddess enveloping
Kali, gauzed thighs in auras of color, pressing dust motes to the core
birthing ghostly beings, half woman half dust

a young girl, just aware of her body, and full
of laughter, skimming the surface of pattern, and full
of laughter
saphire eyes, young girl in the pattern, diamond eyes, the quick
movement to the precise place
marked, not on the stage, but in a young mind, molecules gently
pulsed to a resonance

70

with some dust touched place on resilient boards
untouched nipples, gauzed pale

ebony eyes, prisming light, gentle belly swell at the point of breath
in an instant of stillness
wind machines picking up cast shadows, flute notes
points of breath in darkness, aching, toes landing on wood, flesh
on wood, tiny clicks of five nails on wood, the brush of calloused ball
faint slap of heel ball
the step, piercing and sharp as grass-stained silver
                                    green and silver in the fertile flesh
pulsing heart under shallow breath

one shallow breath, sheet lightning whipping across the flat desire
the dark shrowded flat desert of wanting to reach
shouting my poems from the dark
leaping from the powerful springs in my thighs
in the domed heaven of my skull
moving in astral beauty to the beauty of delicate flesh

she was Earth and brown and green, blue granite veins
and silver and gold and copper and strange metals that rose as she rose
from the seas, flesh and leafy down and leaf mold

                    and i was the wind, when she called
                    the astral current, echoing her flesh
                    borne of her flesh, returned to set the seed
                    we formed together, in our alchemy, into her flesh

Lucifer, fallen star, burned in the heavy air
plunging to the forest
Pan, then, flesh still hot from the fall, pipe full of the song of falling
    thru atmospheres

seat pressing my hot buttocks
molten pills of sweat running down my sides
whole harem twisting, falling, leaping, spiralling up into delicate
                    flames of blue-hot flesh
eyes, precious gems, slicing thru my dark presence

tired poet, high school dancers, mineral thoughts rising up from
primal seas, worn seat underneath, Golden Gloves boxer along side
novelist two rows up, car outside, doughnuts later
but   a head split open to hold dancing currents, hydrogen clouds
of all the eras, recognition of patterns possessing us, bursting out
     of the flesh guises we wear
hungers are Being, full spirits, we are only meat
they wear
the dances, after all, comic or pretty
the dancers, after all, like other girls, pretty or not so pretty
lights harsh, crowd milling, legs a little tired from long sitting, from
     imagining impossible steps in answer
horny old man, dreaming of Gods and Goddesses inventing motion,
     calling it sensuousness, coming to feed on it, ending in flesh
the strange feeling
i'd been   elsewhere

theater unreal, walls fading to sketched outlines
desk and chair and pen metamorphosing into mountain ranges
     and moving grasses

and in this astral realm, i am the wind, touch the flesh without
     a flesh of my own
and i ache to be flesh

THE DESCENT

for Mike Hannon

drop into below

breaking the ice surface
           its reflections

go down where the roots are
           among our coffins

twisted, mud-flaked arms
      thrust down past worms

thru black dirt

     into the dream

         i see the old faces

    laugh, play, move
    about

    until i approach

        then

    pirouette

    into twisted hemp

chords of flame rising, quickly

   used

sudden the static

       smiles

until the dead
rise thru trees

RIVER DREAM

for Jim Cody

High, rocky land.
Places to scramble up
and look out from.
Places to look at, from far off.
Split a rock here and cut into the glistening
                    white
of a seashell.
This thin aired place was under the sea.
When the sea left, shells and the seeds of stone
                    were left,
whole currents
of the sea were left
running from high folds of land
back down to the sea basins.
Talking waters. The rivers
were left.
Clear water? Salt's heavy.
It ran down first. Left clear water
to run through our time.
Saw all this in a drawing of circles in circles
somebody scratched and colored into a stone
where a spring comes out.
Talking waters. The rivers
rushing or falling, half drunk on thin heights,
getting down quick. Getting herded along

on the flats.
Measuring the thinnest grade
with a perking up of the run.
Grab one. Ride it to the whole tangle
we call sea.
Watch the river buck back and forth in its meander.
But old mama Earth
is belly round, folding and humping:
There's an up and down meander, too,
over her gathered flesh.
Might be one somewhere goes clear around her
passing through here and through Cina, too.
Mama Earth is round and fatted up
as a belly
ready to birthe.
Tie that belly up in ribbons.
Crystal blue. Sun-leaf green
or crow green or coyote-eye brown
                all wrapped round
and you got
all the whispering, cawing
        rivers

And it's

                (spring)

HER MAJESTY'S SHIP

for JAMES KENTON BELL

> *to fish ghost waters, to fish*
> *ghost waters for the coal fish*
> —Shaman Song 9

G.F. ODE ROUGH DRAFT FOR AN EPITAPH

For three years, going naked in the streets
Pulling artifacts from a fifth dimension
That would fade in a hostess' sheets,
He attempted to teach the art of suspension—

Disbelief? He'd balance it before your nose,
Pressing the grains together until the solid
Presence was floating about: let your hand close
Around it and feel! Damnable thing sits stolid:

Breathing and sweaty and hot in your tiring hand,
While he is making the others he needs. The pirate
Juggles the pictures as bees would dance, a band
Play, and with heft, opacity, sound, the spirit

Objects gather belief. The man is a thief!
'He paints his poems and writes his pictures'
His Eurydice the future. Often too brief.
Wanting to write our new scriptures!

Offered work clothes imported from Gloucester,
Cap and gown and asylums from Academe,
Magazines, named for the decade, that foster
Career and fame, he went off with his own scheme.

II

The age was one of schools,
A time for fish, not poets.
One must smile, learn the rules.
'If you're not careful, you'll blow it.'

Who wants a rough shod dream dazzled man
And his rough ways?
Better a prize-winning plan
Than strange tunes the inner man plays.

The 'age demanded' something to memorize,
A thing that emulates,
A familiar business to teach, nothing of a size
To suggest cosmic templates.

III

White foam green sea, noisy,
Replaced overtly by factories;
The quick sex of rock
Undoes our subtle Bach.

The Muse's wreath is smoothed
Down, an assembly belt:
Each fad is moved
Along, discarded pelt

From an ossified serpent,
Naga, rough current
Of the sea, rudely spent,
Now, to pay the rent.

The Earth won't allow it,
Said an old man.
A quake —or angry fit
Of the sea? God's ban?

Where are any of these?
The poet is cooked alive.
Slavery hounds the bees
For easy honey in the hive.

It's all a clumsy feast.
Eat lots —and Nat'l Brands.
Tie and cook the beast
Who'd use silvered hands

To make the fine thing.
Make a meal of the dog
Who'd sing sculpted gold
And make the gold ring.

IV

These fought in any case,
      from one end of the office to . . .
and some believing
            what they were told, in any case . . .

Some dark as hawks,
some warlike doves,
some for fake battle,
some for love of the real,
some to win room for the better thing,
most for love of another or gain,
learning later . . .
some in fear, stoning poems lest they be stoned . . .

Carried this war out into its metaphor
            spoke of Asia and men in office . . .
marines with glittering eyes
boy warriors from jungles
circling in mud,
      where poems had been;
rock-faced presidents, inscrutable scholars
where poets had been;
the mud and jungle and corpses painted over auditoriums
      where comfortable 'read ins' were 'in progress' . . .

Everybody came home,
home to the habit of slanting work,
home to the deceit of popularity,
home to the easy job of writing for or against something,

somebody, for prize committees: the ready-made poetry
for ready-made audiences.

Ability as never before, wasted as never before.
The clear eye and juicy loins,
The good lungs and firm voice;

Rhythms as never before,

A place to start as never before,
The rape of the Muse as she'd not been raped before,
Poems half birthed, skewered
And torn apart on the savage teeth.

V

The young, strong haunched
Boys and girls . . .
Their premature children . . .
All dead as careers launched

Careen, smiling toothpaste ads,
Quick eyes gone under cataracts,

For a badly made gold cup
And a place well down on an obscure list.

A WOODEN LEG UP

A woman's goodly flesh
Still had several meanings
When King Charlie said,
Breath for our gleanings.

Flesh less than the panting,
A speaker stands there,
Behind the speaker a story.
And no metaphor.

The diaphragm—
Produces breath, prevents
Unwanted pregnancy.
Poets collecting rents

On rumors of great houses,
The properties never shown.
Breathless reports. Doubt?
That'll get you a groan.

It all happens on the coast.
And a descendent of Ahab.
Poseidon isn't there;
The sea's a Chesire crab.

God's concentric universe
Condemned as artifice,
These New Poets of the Surface
March to a precipice.

'Birthed in one form: died
in another'

Among the proper works and reading lists,
Engaged in smithing a bronze ' wow-hey',
I found the loyal disciple of the
Recentest Boss Poet, Monsieur Copier.

For two hours he waved sacred work;
Of others; of the successful ones;
Told me what the Man (Great) drank
And of his orgies, wives and runs.

The texts, lovingly caressed,
Were not read or quoted,
Were a burden with which he was blessed,
Something to be honorably toted.

The Great Man had kicked every ass
In sight; he'd busted up bars by the dozens.
He'd been in jail, in *Poetry*, too; was New.
Him and Copier was practically cousins.

M. Copier, walking backwards and flushed,
Not needing overly to write,
Bathed by His sun,
Vanished from sight.

BLYTE

The sky-like limping eyes,
The crafty infant's face,
The stilted lecture notes,
Pics —without a song's easy grace.

The heavy book of heaven, yellow pages and one,
Exactly one, given recipe to put
Expression in the face
Of Blyte 'the Decade's Editor.'

MR. REEKSWRATH

In the gilded hall, hot absinthe sipped slowly,
Mr Reekswrath advised absently, back up thunderbolts
With political adroitness,
                         con the dolts.
'I was young as you . . . once . . .
When my juices were hot, I wrote of mountains and mirrors
And married a lot of women . . .
I like to eat; there's art in writing about restaurants . . .
People will READ you, if you catch the popular thing . . .
And compromise'll get you to Europe.

'I've lived years off the post office . . .
Write reviews that get books you can sell,
There's meals in that secret.

'Too many poets about?
Wrap 'em up in a group,
Make a movement of 'em, toss 'em out,
Get rid of the whole troup.

'The renascence has been going
Since the fifteenth century.
To keep on top of the thing,
Keep reviewing the flurry . . .

'But don't tell 'em what's happening,
Tell 'em what happened;
Make the past the present, then the future
Is yours to command.'

.   .   .   .   .

A younger poet: 'Rock's where it's at!
Get you a fine guitar,
Look where everybody's heading at!
Forget your dark old star.'

X

Beneath the sagging roof
The stylist has drunk up his beer,
Unpaid, uncelebrated,
At last from all the goddamned bullshit veneer

Drunkenness saves him;
With a cow-who-never-thought-anything mistress
He exploits his talents
And shitting meets his distress.

His Muse is all the crap that's done to him.
Even asking for a match,

He gets his balls grabbed,
The whole works torn up from their thatch.

XI

She came in from the country,
Posed as a flower child,
Let her hair grow wild:
Still, the calculating gentry.

The deeper sensibilities
Were as a lovely gown,
Bought in the nearest town
To cover her sterilities.

XII

'Daphne with her thighs in bark
Stretches toward me her leafy hands'—
Flower child or Moon Goddess, the age
Doesn't matter if young flesh commands,

But darkened eyes spark and reflect,
Go cool and close,
My flesh is old
To her who chose;

Leaves and bark and blossoms
Naturally grow from her,
She wills them not, wills nothing.
Hers is an easy purr:

She sees herself a queen,
Made of dreams, never to die,
And needs Carnival,
Electric heart-beat, a dulling lie.

Rock in tiny hand, to throw against
Time, the rock she hears—
Rock and light show trip, break
Time, the rocking years—

There is a terrible oldness in the poet.
Reaching to touch her blossoms,
He draws her eye to death in delicate edges,
Her breasts fill with milk, and dry,
Oldness is contagious.

          .   .   .   .   .

But darkened eyes spark and reflect,
Go cool and close,
My flesh is old
To her who chose.

ENVOI (1967)

Her hair was yellow wind, her thigh
The rough hill I danced across.
She put me in her crystal eye
And roped me tight with silver loss.

Her eye is shaped of stars and space,
Each star a cameo alive,
Each cameo a threaded lace
Of days and nights, of hate and love.

These other places, full of men
And women, leaves and rocks and wind,
Are real as any I have seen.
The hands and faces carry histories.

Her hair is nebulae, her thigh
The spreading dark, her pulse the flare
Of novaed suns, of concentric
Universes. My palms are moist.

The darkened softness! Burning visions
Fill me and burn! My stomach in knots
I thrust like rockets to tear the sky!
The spaces suck me up and burn!

I reach to grab the deepest sun,
My back arched and strained to break!
The eye rolls up, clouds and bursts!
My lids unstick and tears roll down—

Tears roll down and wet the sky.
Her white skin and broken leaves
Color the wind and catch my sigh.
A crystal tear on a grass stem grieves.

HER MAJESTY'S

1968

Eisenstein's stone lions in motion

I

Turned from the wine full
And fake spoor
To the tetra head
of architects:
'His Eurydice
The future,'
And his style
The designer's.

Prophesy,
No whole tapestry
His art, but an art
Leading out;

His vision
A squalling infant,
Piss-ants with a hack's bent
Cld laugh derision.

II

invention among the slobs, a fixed image in the mind's eye
'eyes like doorknobs, eyes like doorknobs
'like a statue moving backwards   eyes like doorknobs
   'blinking, blinkin' no
eyes like doorknobs
                    —Mohammed Ali

For three years, an Orpheus who could whale,
He whipped the best lads,
No titles, AKKUSTOM prevails,
Booted out, at last, from that Arcade.

He had thought his gift would mean he had it made.
Among their fixes,
Night Mares fled.

Came up . . . came up from prison late,
Asking time to be rid of . . .
of his DIS figurement; to originate
A new kind of beauty . . .

He had sensed . . . a curtain . . .
(And knew he could tear through) . . . solidify figments—
Came on
With his peculiar pigments:

Unable in the intervening darkness
To see our lusts, his eye finding another
Light, missing what we see,
Seeing its other:

—Given that is his 'one primal passion,'
His need to call our attention
To tear tracks on dusty cheeks
Before new tears erase 'em;

To present the stillness
Of numerous objects in hologram—

He had passed, in rightness, to change,
And set going in rides
The finely drawn riders inside
His soul's range;

He thought to make friends here,
And love dark women deeply:
His gifts crumpled in alien hands . . .
He was charged steeply.

.   .   .   .   .

Not real lions there,
But stone made to live.
The motion not theirs, it's a man's
Eye's the gift to give.

'THE AGE DEMANDED'

From his a-failing to 'read in,'
He was suspected a bit
Of not giving a damn, of Ivory
Towerism, of being unfit.

The shine of hammered gold
Ceased making sense
When it was found
He wasn't doing coins for rents.

He saw a jewel
As though it were a woman . . .
Or, a woman
Transparent as a perfect jewel . . .

And he was asked how this
Got any jobs for the poor or ended war.
He kept believing beauty
Was of direct use, that it would cure.

    The desert erupts everywhere.
    The old men at the water hole
    Refuse to admit they drink air.
    Old rituals are the goal.

Zarathustra laughs at him, rudely.
'I gave 'em poems; they used 'em as diplomas in killing,
They change the arts at will—
They take your form and use their own filling'—

That doesn't release
Him, that faded man
Of the hill, whose brows crease
With lost memory . . .

His ancestors were shamans;
It's locked in his genes.
The proof isn't there to show,
But he'll find the means . . .

Somehow . . . the reason Homer lives, while men
He sang of died, like lights blinking out . . .
A man dying again
In each memory into which he'd stepped . . .

'Burn, baby, burn!'
One glittering man cursed another.
He, of course, burned
Always . . . as no other . . .

The 'age demanded' very simple plots,
The good and the bad clearly
Marked; of course, lots
Of his work would *do* . . . nearly.

Deep concern of self-styled 'his betters'
Leading, for his own good,
To his being . . .
Ah . . . nudged aside by the go-getters.

IV

A savage victim head,
His Earth is terribly shrunken.
It's no great task, to step around
The whole drunken

Global vine-tangle of humanity.
The toy forests
Grind patiently
To sand . . .

And night is a shadow, to step
Into, out of, at will—
Not the dark fear his fathers held—
The ocean's a great still . . .

But he's a God
And drinks the sun
That'll prod
His heart to a run,

Saving the sea-green seas
For a quieter hour;
He'll drink them through his teeth
And catch a sea-green lover.

'It's all a-birthing and a-dying,
Always, and both at once—
And when it's small enough and crying,
I'll take it up at once'—

HOLOGRAM

Turquoise blouse
In the sun
Pales her skin,
Turns her hair copper,

The copper's conductivity
Filling the first breath
With lucidity,
With a flaming wreath;

My hand is taken, white
Fingers, firm water
Leading my touch
To the slaker

Of thirsts, and thirsts
Remain, wait
Through the slaking,
The thirsts.

Her eyes are twin moons
Under the sun . . .

THE LAST ANCESTOR

A con man in the thirties
with no greed.
He used his dark charm to get a job
past men grumbling in lines.
One paycheck in a broad hand
— then, the binge.
Money gone, the smile
would come out of the hangover
and he'd reach for the next job.
I figure he had a rich Louisiana accent
and got mean when he was drunk and scared.
Rough clothes.
Something in me not yet memory
tells me
the rasp of rough clothes.
The last time he thumbed a truck
or grabbed a freight
and spit out the dust of Stockton
or Oakland
i hadn't learned how to see
a human face.

3 MEDITATIONS

i

"Eskimos have 17 words for snow . . ."

monks ask

ancient master
    eyes reflect
        quick rivers
    teeth are sharp
    knotted hands
      hold sticks

where is buddha

long fingers

       peach pits
bent trees
cattle droppings
striking with sticks

there is buddha

my time came to ask
the question came

where am i

              peach pits
bent trees
cattle droppings
striking with sticks

call back
what you have sent out

buddha

          ii
              "If you try to see me through my form,
               or if you try to hear me through my
               voice, you will never reach me and will
               remain forever a stranger to my teaching"
                                —Gautama Siddhartha

a stone
sits in the stream
a sound of passing

          iii
              "I had a dream last night
               I don't understand my dream
               But i know everything is all right, now"
                                —an inmate: San Quentin, 1958

i am back

where do you think
you have been

here

NEGRITUDE

where
     you goin
all
dressed up
    an smilin

dark flats ona
      wall

matchin me step
       by step

       i'm black
          now
      didn't go lookin
         t'be
      black was born
      pink   blue pools
      drinkin it in

back   back now
      back in

   sane trainer
crackin
whys

WHORE

i

she undressed slowly
with a sense
of the moon among clouds
stretched
to take up the belly's
beginning slack
snapped out the saffron bulb
to silhouette herself
beside the moon
she copied

ii

she washed off
her cunt
with the slow care
of a craftsman
for his tools
fingering the lips
figuring the years

she rung out
her wash rag, twisting
worn threads
dry

ATHENA

Recess.
The children running,
cries and laughter
bouncing
down the halls,
bursting into the yard—
a girl with dark hair
running
into the wind,
looking about,
tasting the wind,
running to play
her game, hop-
scotch, running
to find a stick to draw
the lines,
a *tor* to throw.
She throws back
her head, eyes
sparkling in the wind.

The other girls
hopping madly, falling,
toppling over
and laughing,
the patterns painted
on asphalt;
a girl with dark hair
playing
alone, scratching
thin lines in naked dirt, eyes
glittering in a quiet
face as clouds
shadow her try.

She throws back
her head,
her nostrils dilate.

The sky goes slowly
dark—
the children scent
rain, laugh
and watch the sky.
A girl with dark hair,
whose eyes
glint in a dark face,
throws the *tor*—
the sun, gone now,
there is no wind.
She looks up, eyes glitter,
an age comes, and a need.
She lifts one foot,
holding the scuffed shoe
in a sure hand,
the ritual maiming exciting
the intent face
of a journey.
The sky darkens.
The children fall slowly
back—
a girl with dark hair
bouncing
wends a careful way:

> *Court the distances.*
> *Leap, find the chances.*
> *Count the instances*
> *and learn the dances.*

the sky closes in.

DAPHNE

I walkt, glass in hand,
thru cocktail
parties

studied the protean masks of Daphne
reflected in the waters
of the magically replenishéd glass.

I nibbld onions & olives

      —casually toucht the bark
admired the seasonal flowerings.

I tasted laurel in theater lobbies

& thought   often   how different
these fastidious wreathes
on tuxedoed arms   lookt

from olive flesh running
under an afternoon
sun.

MARRIAGE

for Hilary

i trace your lip

in the quiet

crystal glasses unused
smiling engraved faces

not there

just the quiet

and a ring that fits

exactly

COMPOSER

*I wake
in the morning,
turn over,
hear your piano,
know
the piece
from other mornings,
but not the name.
Like it*

and listen.

Right then
I don't much care
that you
steal
my butter and cereal

and think poets
are second-
class,
should carry out
your
garbage,

while you dream
of cocks
and virile youths
who pretend
mindlessness and come
mystically
in your mouth
and midnights
you buy
with subtly perverted
music.

You miss a note
but I
don't even notice.
I'm sleepy
deep in images
of a chick
I met at a concert.
And the piano
makes it
like a movie.

COLORS OF LOVE

You look up
from our book (its pages

well thumbed)

& your tears
        grow restless
in the burnt sienna room
our love
fashioned.

Beautiful young men with
homely faces
        thread tapestries

on guitars
        tapestries that color
your breasts with deep
blues, chinese reds,

tapestries to show you
a copper sun
over flowers gently played
        (whose leaves speak

softly to your running feet)

& your tears

                restless
in the burnt sienna room,
silent
at its windows.

EULOGY

The room
soundless, is larger than before.
The paper is impersonal.

Footsteps, laughter,
the light voice: I love you.
The register is wrong;
The sound doesn't touch the room.

The dust motes wait
for an exhaled breath to move them.
The paper, too, will yellow.

EUCALIPTI

for Leslie Johnson

A breathing hidden.
Leaves crinkle, pale shells fall.
Leaf patternings pressing into my arm.
Another man's woman; i can't reach to touch.
Sun centering a ring of tree tops. Shadow writhing.
Is she really there? I never touch anything
of my world anymore. Light splatters.
"Penguins are birds. They fly in the water."
I spread my arms.
I fly through fallen leaves.
Her hands, gliding Japanese paper, hold
pearl grey shells; deep vessels
with sectioned lids over
maroon caves. Vein patterns in decaying leaves
fine as lace; her forehead, pale blue threads, sky tracks
of bird flight.
Afternoon is minute rustlings
touching a thicket.

THE WORDS

I carry boulders across the day
From the field to the ridge,
And my back grows tired.
A few, stubborn, in a field drawn
To old blood by the evening sun
And trembling muscles, remain.
These chafe my hands,
Pull away into the black soil.
I take a drop of sweat
Onto my thumb,
Watch the wind furrow its surface,
Dream of a morning
When my furrows will shape this field,
When these rocks will form my house.
Alone, with heavy arms,
I listen thru the night to older farms.

BREAKS

33 1/3

fingers
      on strings

         for mingus

pink touches
         & brown
     movement
     rape

harlequin's beat
         of
     celestial

time   reshape

it into a cruel
         heat

     of organic
     times

the riff is born

45

her songs
fast

tumble head
first

      out
      over plas
tic egos

jar

her voices
loose

she hunts shy

in
side for her
face

78

raspberry for critics

hobo
      ride

set sail

take it
       wide

thru a hole
dream of bride
thru a hole

in a fence
          tall

leave ole dick

wonder   wonder

how i stick
         the side

that slippery

hobo car

33 1/3—stereo
dialog for saxaphone and trumpet

i
kali

grey feet
dance

a feral
threat

wear past
thin
surfaces

eat ex

posed
hearts

ii
siva

toes
cascade

light
sprinkle

fall
ing

abruptly

shatter all the

eyes

THE SONNET MAKER

for John Ratliff

child playing
shadow on a wintered beach

scratching
delicate lines
in this grey green sand

inviting
unseen
rivulets of the sea
under changeless cliffs

to shape
rows and tandems of boxes
in which the maimed king

will dance
his one footed dream

he throws his found taw

thoughtless
of the variations

he asks

305 HONDA

for Gary Snyder

Leaving a forest of bikes,
leaving the university, headed for San Francisco.
  [after watching the wistful look
    at a different set of handlebars, a wider grip,
    a deeper control]
Leaning into the curve, sliding along the arm
of inertia,
settling into the traffic, edging around it,
headed for San Francisco.

Move forward, hold onto me, not the bike.
Find the center
of gravity,   the Buddhist
Oneness & uniqueness.
Leaning against the arm of the curve.
Two poets   personal perceptions
one rider, multi-armed, -legged.
Point of intimacy:
from the first tools,   crafts,
metals & men laboring, hot, sweat
wetted, laboring with flesh & minds.
Fires & dreams, fires & gradually the machines.
The long sight.
The whole technology, a series
of carefully timed openings, man with his fire
manipulating the frozen rhythms
of road surfaces,
the intricate network of wind-rivers, the falls,
lurches,   sudden eddies.
A line of intended movement.

Be loose & heavy
against the movement's changes.
The changes—
we throw our movements out,   read them
& prophesy.

Along a bay-shore highway,
wind falling loose, snapping tight with a whipped
crack at my ear, past drift-wood sculptures
on mud-flats —a sailing ship, a
locomotive, a huge & angry Indian—
movie sets, but with a looser texture, allowing
the different movements of sea & sky to show thru.
Past —leaning to the curve, headed for the tollgate
& the rise of the bridge.

A quarter given, a brief touch of a stranger's
hand, shoulders moving in front of me
& the bike jumping up over the bay, drawing
the winds into the center—
the bay like any sea, the lands rushing into the
center,
the carefully timed movements of man & his fire.

The other poet calling
back
over his shoulder
the voice cut loose, drawn thin,
wavering,   snapping past my ear.
Gone.   Missed.
A strange wind-eel, wavering, curious,   vanished.
The silent wind-eels crawling like ropes
over my forehead, thru my hair, down my neck.
Vanishing.

Wind-eels edging around my glasses, pulling
at them.   Testing my vision.
Crawling into my eye-sockets, changing the shape
of things seen—
the shape-changers, the wind-flowing
& sounds of rice-paddy girls
& distances.

The bridge supports reach up,
drop back, & the wind rushes down, pushes at us,
keeps up its peculiar chants & animal cries, comes
out of the void & sings of the invisible planets,
suns, distances; & the changed landscape sits
in its new perspectives, indifferent
to the wind-rivers, silver & muted violets, the poems

at the edges of the bay
large shapes at the edges of the bay, chiseled
out of light
                    the rough sketches, reaching out of
sight, nature's poems   & the clumsy rectangles
& silent windows of man's
the edges of the grounds carefully surveyed, the hours
of construction computed, paid for.
The cathedral chants of the wind; we lean to the curve,
falling into the shadow
of the city. Our sound larger, now, than the wind-river's.
Words coming back,
& a heaviness, & the old geometries carrying us over
subdued hills;
falling into the shadow & headed
for a vodka martini.

JAZZ IMAGES

1

run down
        green

the trail, run down
the green trail
past the end of day

red   red   red

goats

on a ridge
under purple and blood

        sky

2

tin cans in the compost
       of the dump

almost silver
almost silver

rolling streaks molten
        silver

the reflection

her turning glasses

3

> round and hairy
round hairy notes, notes
yellow and brown in early
> morning
mist
of cigarettes

> swamp souls
coming out, out at me

thru, thru my ears, to the
> dark places

where wild creatures ran

before the smoke

4

roll
roller coaster street

> ooohhh
it's all rises and quick
> falls

see 'em jiggle, up—
thrust breasts and balanced buttocks

they're fit
in tight print dresses

> and then others

ain't

ain't fit for print

5

dance of cold fire
      on the winter ocean

grey sun floating
melting into green black seas

a marshmallow collapsing
      into the hidden

brown heat

of hot
hot chocolate

frozen night played under

     muted gulls

6

   bury the fire
wrap it up, late
at night

deep olive cocoons
warm as mom's womb

smoothing out lumps
of closed-hard ground

watch shooting stars

drops of cosmic rain

FIRE FALL

Your eyes
green against the fire light
brown
         at other times
         in other lights

earth—
but green tonight
soft jungles

And I lie upon you
my hands curving to your shapes
against the carpet   one side
warmed   reddened   the other in shadow

night sounds

Behind your breath-suspended
smile
jungle sounds

And the fire
         coals   forgotten

EUROPE

eyes, smoky crystals,
deep smoke, moving, trying to shape,
   all the songs are lost songs,
   all thoughts are memories, dying,
around the eyes she waits
knowing i must come out of the eyes,
content to wait,
  she told me her name and i forgot
  she touched my hand, beads of moisture
holding us apart,
  infinitesimal pearls of water
fire-walkers step upon,
    'you don't know me,'
'but of course i know you,'
  'no, you can't know me,
  'i am a mystery,
  'i am not knowable,'

folding grey smoke, stories unfold,
   around the stories are names,
   relatives, clamouring to speak,
   old smiles, stripped from mirrors,

'i was Miss World in 19. . .
   'i haven't danced since i was young,
   'pretty, Miss World, all those things,
'would you dance with me,
'come out of my eyes and dance,
  'let me walk again on fire,
  'love my outside, leave me alone,

  'to smoke in peace . . . .

PRIMER

see

the city
the city
is
full of
cops

they're
turning
up waste
baskets

bed
clothes

old
bottles

looking
looking
thru
the city

for dope

what
will they
do
when
they find

i
turn on
with
just

poems

HELL ODE

magic spells come off our lips
soap bubbles drifting away
from innocent children

or air split foam from rope
lips of madmen frenzied
by erupting dreams

apples are eaten by naked figures of our thoughts

soft
to wear well, shadow
stained skin curls inward
surfaces of dreams, taut
as glass, or

when we're admitted, a slow
swimming

wizards
constructed a pentagon
the radial rotations humming

invoked
the spirit of war

an apple may come a fiery crystal emitting music
the crazed eye of vision

rolling day into night in a cramped
net of universe filling the wind
with silver compass points

grey flesh of human bodies
collecting in wild lament
the ruined light

the red earth is swallowed by youths at the edge of dawn

                        cut
               of bright teeth, spurted
                    blood gushes in a lava flow
                    molten surfaces of dream
               as glass, or

                    the hot white, stained red
                    swimming

          wizards
     constructed a hexagon
                         two lobes touching

          encircled
     the spirit of bees

the firewalker's secret, silver balls of sweat
     the mirror eye of secrecy

          the soft faces of children
               moist blurs of white
     molten roll of translucence
               before the red stain
     the soft faces of children
               keys to the dream

GLIMPSES OF A COLD NIGHT

a film scenario

window steamd white
a dinner table
         and one chair

           *

       seven wooden steps
         two shoes
       tap-tap   tap-tap

  *

tiny white clouds
in battle
boy and girl laughing

         *

       crumpld letter
          blowing down a street
       absolutely still
       old crumpld man

  *

grey mist laughing
    friends
thru foggd glasses

THE STRANGER

I found a panther
in the streets of San Francisco.

Lost, hungry,
he eyed me as a menace; & I was.

I have stomped panthers
to death,
torn open their bellies,
eaten their blood—
soaked entrails in the dark
streets of San Francisco; & in other cities

I have led panthers
when I was lost, hungry; they were my menace.
They ate my blood—
wetted entrails under the street lamps
of their cities.

HARVEST

i come upon stones
in the wind shoved grasses

they wait
tensed
curled in on themselves

i reach out to touch
sun warmed quiet and flame
jumps to scorch my fingers

i suck on my burnt hand
and look to the far circle
of mountains
brothers to the stones

my hurt fingers tell me
grey silences i cannot touch
were once my messengers

ΨΥΧΗΔΗΛΟS

i

silver backing flakes from the mirror, falls

bright snow

from the direction of the Pleiades

each platinum faceted pellet

coming down
fast as light

i catch them
with the grace and shout of a riveter

in a molecule thick membrane of hand

a hand filling the evening sky

at my equator—

ii

outside my room a darkness

the trick   there is always a trick

is in keeping an equalized pressure

change it just a bit

the skin of the room   waves like flags joined

along their edges

shape a floor
to the texture of a lovely girl
lie on her

if you can-can

if you can-can

    iii

Moon-woman laughs

        a harmonium at play

her breasts are cones
ice cream spilling over

        sticky

threads lacing stars together

      O, Moon-woman
      turn from the window

      only a darkness
      lies beyond my room

      there is nothing to await

    and i am the great riveter

how much, in gold
coin, so i may carry your child

her nipples were gold coins

swollen to suns
in her quick pregnancy

    from across the raging room

      was our only way to love

i threw out my love
and when i missed, great furrows

            were cleaved in her flesh

      but when those silver pellets struck

        she would throb and swell

and 300 things
would come to be in my room

     iv

Sun-man, armed with the compleat angle -er

       explores in my room

    the room is rectangular
    by measure
    a block of oleomargarine

    sliced into thin sheets
    it is a Holy Book

    the light-globe people
    are writing in it

        their dazzling heads
        melting the pages together

    bright heiroglyphs
    lost in chunks of hardened
    Greece

       Sun-man rocks on fat buttocks
      popping globes with silver rocks

i collect fragments
trying to read
over exploding shoulders

v

        the crone
read my palm, scraping away calluses
      saving them
            in a stone jar

your life-line
is hollow-stump peculiar
dark-kitten irregular

however i rede
wherever i pick it up
it leads to the four corners
of the room

you must, my dear
pulling my hips from me, jarring
them with the calluses

      you musk, my dear
          flared nostrils bat-flying
            thru the strands of room

     feel a map
     lest you forget this room
     when the magic physic
     is done
     and you shrink to solid-state

uncallused fingers
sorebright from cracked safes

weave life-lines
thru points of light

with a quick stitch
and a soaking up of colors

129

vi

      Sun-man is lecturing upon
litters and scions

        advancing into awlcomy

        the equator is one who equates
        the equated an equature

        in the beginning was . . .

    teacher, tell us of the equinox
tell us   again   of the lovely equinox

        equinox is the coroner stone
        the frowndation
        of awl dumbocracy

        a contraction of 'equal knocks'
        —for awl
awl is an only bard of murdern kratosism

    vii

WARNING

      all mining must be confined to the interior

          the skin of the room
        may be pushed back, arranged variously
         but must not be torn

              or darkness will spill in

      reductive mining is recommended

the miners are brawny fellows
cyclopian

corneal lamp peering deep in

to dig   what is kneaded
without cutting threads of the map

there are many bits of pellet-element
all held apart by chunks of rock
the task of the miner, to ask

the bits to move inward from the rock shell
and form an arrangement one might enter

the miners expose their veins

i wear the bright colors

viii

mirror, mirror
on the wall

who is

billowing clouds of cotton candy

must be packed into tiny ore-cars
for delivery

the skin of the room hides

behind thickness, a sickness

builds in my hope

Sun-man is gone, out the window

Moon-woman is dead

the old crone in her lace of answers

retreats to a corner

of the ceiling

silver comets fly to the mirror

and strangers entering the room

are opaque

SONNET 3

Oh, singeth thee the gentle chunes
Of love! And let thy voices guide my pen
To make a flaming thread to weave again
The fiery net that trappeth lovers' runes
And make of them our songs! The yellow noones
Have burnèd greenery, dried our sea-ken;
And thou hast gone to some unfindable den.
And I am left with burnèd flesh on the dunes.
Oh, I have writ the songs of old,
Revivèd forms and words and ways of speech.
And I have callèd forth the sea and drowning.
And loving work maketh desert a beach.
But critics say I sound like Mrs. Browning,
And *avant gardists* fear my soul is sold.

SHARDS FROM THE SONG

I

My love of you is a sun !

A very old thing to say.
Lately, though, we've come to know
of suns !

A burning plasma held in invisible fields !

And if those fields break, will the brief fires
of our lives be consumed, drifting ash be our touching?

II

Old men do not hunt the wild deer.
The strength is there, in gnarled old muscles under softened flesh,
and if the eye is weakened slightly, there's more mind within it,
but one's star-whitened image in her eye consumes the spirit.

        Old men do not hunt the wild deer.
They dream of its light step
patterned softly in the roaring winds
of high plains,
where young men flash like lightning
on the soft runner's trail.

Still, an old man scenting the wild deer
might rage against the Law,
freshen his meat to youth, drinking blue light from high pools,
run again on the springing arch of time

and touch the shoulder of the wild deer.

III

We touch as uneasy guests touch priceless crystal.
Light plays in the cut facets, full colors and dizzying fumes make
      us wild,

and we wonder at the thought of drinking.

The lights in the great hall are harsh
and the slightest shudder might explode the crystal.

IV

We wear protocol
            as a kind of radiation clothing
so that, passing near
one another,
we will not 'spark'
and leave ionized signals
to wake those who sleep nearby.

V

In dark places i have made a mirror.

                Bright purple, this mirror
of gold-aluminum alloy,

a mirror for my darkening passion, and another the
living green of gold-iron,

                for the freshness of something fresh borne
in me, a growing light that is you,

and in these mirrors, i watch
through all the hours and am shown the bright play
of your deep fires
so long as they burn.

And none of these mirrors show me the child
i'm told you are.

They show me a living field rising in warm amber

            the fire becoming flesh.

ATTHIS

Recollection lies still
and restless.
Atthis came near to us.
She splintered light
        with her taut silver skin,
casting shadows of strange color
into the marble discs
under our coffee cups;
among the blue-white eyes
her eyes were bronze hyperions.
Candles spit
into night; coffee darkens;
i should be thinking of where
i'll sleep when night's cold
comes in the dark, not where
this glimpsed pale slip will
be lying asleep.

OBSIDIAN

a pilgrim's processional

"your poems carved from obsidian"
A way of telling me
I have the Evil Eye.

Cut away from poet scenes. Di-vision.
Nobody is left to talk to.
Slumping in Hardcastle's coffee house. Die vision.
Can't get it out.
Not the landscape wasted, Mr. E.
Me wasted, image chained in the center of my head.
My monastery: place of singled star.
"Man" s p e l l e d backward is "nam(e)."

Unhoused and living on sidewalks.
Walking all night; watching for the sun.
Hello Helios!
Food over Berkeley hills, an eating of pure light.
On sight: loosing belly snakes
held tight lest space winds suck the last crawling
      into their black draft,
the sun coming yellow obsidian.

No winter in Berkeley
according to the sleepers behind streamed windows.
Blood running silver
in my 3:00 a.m. veins.
6:30 a.m.   yellow-brown iodine stain
turn my head inside out
a flower opening.

Midnight coffee house closure
ejecting mumbling freaks into the night,
Venus long gone   earlier a diamond tip
on the moon's horn. Mars hot.
Walked night sidewalks
hunting poems in the greyed, grainy stuff.
Walking night sidewalks
                              now
for lack of a bed's rent
feet fading into the grey blocks.

Walk diametered night.
Walk against being busted for having no place to go.
Walk to shove blood through slowing serpent body.
Walk to get away from each spot as it takes on the smell
      of my death place.
Sidewalk mania
fingers tipped
into wet cement
years earlier,
glyphs deciphering into
"return to go."

Mist.
Glasses evolving into ice.
I look out through frozen waterfalls.
Owl telling me: "Get off my turf."
Beak shattering the water.

Color sucked from the flowers
by vampire night. Night underneath
teeth sunk in pores.

Watch beat slamming my wrist
breaking up my pulse
sending its spiked blows
to cramp my heart.

Along sides of the street
see-mental squares
in mazed sequence
for a poet's sightings.
My ghost going back to a coffee table and
     warming ghost hands around a wavering cup,
telling the Virginia Slim girl
against a burlap coffee bean sack,
"I'd take yeh home
an' fuck yeh into smoke, jinn;
but livin' like I do
I've lost my ki."

Stoned on cold.
Window's echoed light a man of blue granite.

Wanted, from the beginning, to teach.
To reach a poetfinger (nonelectric brainprobe)
into the quiet cells
and waken the fine hairs, the nerve hairs,
     the light-drafting edges.
Secret of Jupiter: induce flow.
Nothing thrown. All done with mirrors.

Helios!
The pyre amid the ghosts in my senses.
My feet are numb and numb the two legs.
My back is numb and time, gone numb, stops its flow.
A wooden bench melts to velvet.
A magnet of velvet tugging at my back, flesh drawn out
     from my rib cage
but lying down is a bust, a sun-burst of cop
in dark arrest.
Demon screeching under the street lamps
of his city.

Thick maple light in Mel's drive in
     and golden waffles to soak it up,

if pocket lint were gold.
Stopped hands of the watch just above my stopped hand.
Blood running silver
in my 3:05 a.m. veins.
6:30 a.m.   yellow-brown vomit stain
stomach heat
a seared line in the sky.

My ghost going back to a coffee table and
    warming ghost hands on a wavering white dwarf,
silvered see-mental squares
against burlap windows.
Water gas under grey coat.
Water gas under grey skin.
Water gas under grey nerve lining.
Breathing an icy placental water
    cold belly of a bitch muse.

Blood running silver.
'Lectric pain.
3:47 a.m. 'lectric vein.
6:30 a.m. platinum sky
gold tears fry
turn my head inside out
my hand on a cold dawn.

Night is 300,000 steps
on spongy knees
under broken lips and icicle nostrils.
Dawn is pale piss.
Everybody out and hurrying, hands in coat pockets.
And it's warm enough
to sleep on wet grass
Dreaming a woman's warm belly
and smell of breakfasts
while ants crawl in my eyes.
Uncarved obsidian.

KITCHEN

A skein of dull silk.
This knot we call life unravelling
so we can hold
it in the eye;
make it a lesser mystery.
Or a hope.
The bulb welds dust into armor:
Light doesn't rush —
it drips, a kind
of drool off monstrous lips
drying and flaking down
like the paint.
My dark lover, driven farther and farther
back into the house,
the kitchen as far as she could go,
painted a self portrait
in the flaking paint,
colored chalk and the chalk
vision,
pouting lip,
face swollen with the netted scream,
hair greened,
face paled
and swollen.

The paint coming off
dull chips
and the bared strata of paints and papers
and muck turning to oil or coal.
And the cracks —
An evolving map, pre-Columbian
made from the air,
proof of alien beings beating us to the survey,
anticipating Turkish admirals
and wall-gazing poets
and dark lovers driven back
and immortals
demanding the latest news
and kitchen-gardens
where we
grow.
Unravelling.

THE FLOWERING CACTI

Chin tucked into collar.
Red and white eyes rolled up
into steel blue sockets.
Scruffy rooster cackling in my throat.
Unhired. Unhinged.
Derelict with a few poems in print.
Arms folded, back bent,
trying to keep my belly warm.
Squeaking doors in that belly.
Too stubborn to admit
all the poets are dead,
I keep croaking, "Some of us
are only dying."

SHAMAN DRUNK

A swallow cuts the sky in two
and cacti are stopped in warriors' salute.
Up out of dream
layers and hollows and
more layers
above the land.
City bred.
A long sighting down time
to first shamans
and out into time against planet hopping shamans
and star hunting shamans.
Wine on the terrace at Enrico's.
Neons hinting at possibilities of Naked Truth.
Vision rises out of the flames
where my crotch is flush
against the woman's crotch
— jammed trees —
Earth is quaking and ripping and panting
and howling.
A meditation method
for Coyote.
Hunkered down flatfooted and holding
onto my knees in an unfurnished room
no different
from a stone age man
and still seeing things
i can't make sense of
can't handle in any way
but to bring back in song
against a time
they'll be useful.

NAME DREAM

Old at 40?
"Fowler ain't no shaman."
Which of those quick women in the poems
did i *actually* meet?
Might even still be a virgin.
Belly still.flat.
Feathers in the crack of my ass.
Sun blooded mountains painted on my eyeballs.
"All those stones in your poems.
You ever build a stone house?
Like Jeffers?"
Thing is . . . the words
keep raising blisters on my hands.
"Fowler ain't no shaman."
Who says i can't have a name dream
every 48 hours?
And nail that sparrow hawk
on the wing.

REDWING BLACKBIRDS AND OTHER FAUNA

redwing blackbirds and other fauna

for Paul Foreman

All the *forma,*
> eh, amigo?

They see one of us cross the sky

> just shake their heads,
didn't see a thing.

Want their *love,* of course.
And i've been taught, brought up right, know
i gotta be the *same*
every time they *look at* me.

> Poet-light flares,
the world gets dim
and i forget.
Awkward,
not being able to stay in one form,
> mountain lion
> prowling down a city street
wolf
edging through a coffee house

> mocking bird, sitting
on the king's shoulder.

A *stylus* taken to the edges.
Call it writing; it's more like cutting away corns

                    on the edge of a foot
that goes to hoof,
right on your damned palm.
Call it singing; it cracks space, and shatter-lines
gather up
and figure, and the figure walks
                    across the sky, blood-winged
and horny,
and there i am, again, sixty feet up
                    in trouble
roots sprouting
from my wing tips;
coffee getting cold below.
Poems ruffling.

BALLERINA

for Morton & Lynn Grinker

It ain't fair.
Y'know, it ain't fair.
She moves up there, in divine
ballistics,
leg muscles are bow strings,
tits almost nonexistent,
and a *Geist* in her that reaches clear through
and grabs just under my ribs,
a delicate squeeze, with child hands,
a vice,
and all breath is gone.
And my surrogate.
There, him, he's me, y'see,
just for the audience, because
i'd fall on my ass
and ye'd die of embarassment,
in the box, wanting
to applaud your friend, so
he's there,
reaching out toward her,
carrier for my terrible, white-hot lust,
echoing her coolness,
but all he does
is lift her up, offering her
to some stage hand above the curtain,
or God, or
some Geist,
and he puts her down,
glances to see if his cod-piece is straight
and waltzes off.
My ass is spread on the chair,
yours, Mort, embracing the chair,
and yours, Lynn, attractive on the chair.
And up there

the better reflection of me is waltzing off.
And, balancing on one toe,
defying gravity *and* me,
                    she looks out of her
terrible, vulnerable, lovely
mask,
the mask of a young girl, mouth
slightly tight, eyes lightly
moving,
a Goddess, looking toward some God, wanting
a rape
no mortal can deliver.
Ballet?
A divine ballistics, terrible wrenchings
of human musculature,
only the faintest trace of sweat, a gleam
on her forehead,
a slow drop down the line of her lowest rib,
a trace of wetness
at the crotch line of her suit,
the scent far off;
through the mask
eyes are looking so far
the edge of their sight blinds any fool
enough to get close
and do anything more than
lift her,
offering her briefly
to whoever is up there,
and waltz off.

THE BRIDGE

A tramp-clown high on a tightrope
                              wine high

            faces turned up
                        white and split

            open, howls

                        laughter
                        from black pits
                        bubbling up
                        red and thin.

                  Every act

            a bridge

over-sized shoes
                        in desperate search

            for a rope

that in the best of times

                        is only a figment.

            I'll wobble a bit.

      That'll get 'em
                        all worked up.

            But i won't fall
            you greedy devils

                              bin staggerin'

            along this rope

            pushing out strands

            since time began

"GOD DIDN'T MAKE HONKY TONK ANGELS"

for Jim Bell

Nostalg!
The game —always lookin' back
t'see.
The "fifties" painted
onto the "seventies" in one, stupendous
over-wash,
guar-an-teed to bring a tear.
Sittin' knees up
against the seat in front,
chewin' popcorn, watchin'
people flattened out ona screen
an' Hank Williams
sound trackin' outta
radios on truck seats an' otter sech
in *The Last Picture Show.*
The "fifties"?
Well, y'know i spent 'em
on Okinawa,
sweatin' and rottin',
an' in San Quentin, worryin'
over a gut-ful o' time, for
practicin' the trade
the Army taught me,
but in 1959, in a skid road hotel,
a Harlan county gal, lookin' about
fourteen, sittin' in a bathtub,
knee to knee with me, singin'
her heart out, an'
watchin' me, outta the edge o' her
eye, soundin'
like the gal on the record
you allus played when i came over
for beer,
you know,

Kitty Wells,
an' i didn't remember,
'til you footnoted my article on the hotel
(nostalg) that "God didn't make Honky Tonk
Angels" —or *what* the song was!
Or know where Harlan county went.
And Kitty Wells is singin' again
these days
and she don't sound like
a green-eyed gal in a bathtub
a-tall.

NIGHT DESERT

Sun glare left over
out of the dream,
street lamp
framed in the window.
Roll over, put my hand on
a moist haunch
— sprouts an arm
to pat me
dismissingly.

Mist around the moon.
Rain tomorrow.
Mist around the street lamp.
Rain any minute.
Sun glare burns gristle out of sockets;
desert sand shifts,
                    flowing
in slow motion currents
through flesh.
Cup a warm breast.
Evoke a shove.
Keep changing. If you lie down
among the visions
you'll never get up.
They'll find bleached principles
along the roadside
or in a gully
miles from any road
or on gritty flatness where even winds
twist down into gasps.
The last white bone
catches the glint of light —
moon — lamp — sun.
The roadside drifts around
always pointing
another
way.

COSMIC LANGUAGE

Walking.
Lifting a foot and falling
forward, eye
hovering and darting.
A good swinging walk.
Prowling outward, birthing change,
climbing over
the long curve of the globe, while flesh
lets go,
skin sags over into pockets,
eyes swim.
Blue green flashes hover and dart
over shadowed bronzing
of copper's orange glare,
dragonflies
flagging the far inward curve of world.
Restless breezes touch my nostrils,
iced sea winds raging
outward,
curving in the far mist
and raging again
inward
and through me.
Cities fall away
and rain forests, deserts, mountains,
coiled and holding rivers, after looming over me,
and dried out, half caved away footprints,
from which grasses spring back,
and the grasses,
ship grooves and the waters
rushing back into them.
It all falls away,
falls out into distance
and curves

inward,
rushing through me.
All my walkings.

An opening *night journey* through San Francisco,
cavorting
in and out of the *personae*
of my predecessors
                      tickling infant lines
into mime.

A closing one in Berkeley,
hunger gnawing reflections out of concrete.
Corpse rolling
through the rhythms, turning
on its spit.
Again and again.
Walking.
Nothing so simple as a city.
Or rain forest. Or desert. Or mountains.
Walking, now, with eyes open
to themselves.
Where do i put my foot?
Nothing there til it's placed.
The *power.* Never thought upon.
Used easily, when used, by all of us.
Doing it consciously? Hideous.
How many times to fall and get up and fall?

Amid fallen leaves
                     piled against the curb,
a *stone*
sparkling brightly with a quiver
of beginning life.
                     An unseen thing.
Called upon to summon it
school children twist in tortuous

agonies of mumbling
praxis.
Lapis philosophorum.
Black marks on the white sheet.
Nothing there but marks, tracks of articulating
bird-foot.
No meaning. No message.
'Til the outpouring of an eye.
In that outpouring, the secret of our *power.*
The *stone*
cast out, to fall and roll in the leaves,
to blood leaves' edges,
to leap
and become light.
                        Network of light leapings.
We cast a net
outward in a great swirling disc of flight,
cosmic fishermen,
and haul in our load of order.
But our *power?* The order we net is our own,
sent out
and hauled back.
Nothing seen that the eye didn't make.

Walking.
Seeing nothing but what i dream,
touching nothing not of my invention,
smelling only
stray odors of my own passing,
hearing musics rising from my own sources, my *muses.*
Nothing.
No *thing* that isn't a man,
isn't me.

"Don't read things into what's there!"
There's nothing there, no there, but for my reading.
And how much dare i read?

What the Hell, why not
all of it?
And reading, i'm
walking.

coda: A sea
         washes around my feet, echoed
         in currents of running sand, and
         half sunk, embedded in green-grey mush
         the half-rotted skull
         of some prehistoric man, some pre-man
         or *ur*man,
         ants, who once dreamed of flesh-bits,
         petrified juttings of the bone.
         A *recognition.*
         How achingly long, this walk.
         The waters tugging at ankle hairs.
         The sands skillfully slipping out
         from underfoot.
         There's nothing there, no there, but
         for my reading.
         Lifting a foot and falling . . .

RUSHLIGHT

for Amelia

I search for the city
in grey ocean fogs that turn light
back into my eyes
where it lies, waiting to reach out again.

And in this center place
with its faceted windows and white walls
and springing greenery,
i rest past your grin

into your enfolding arms
and curving belly, hearing songs echo
through a small amber light
spinning away

from your eye
to shadow through
this aerie.

ANCESTORS

*on reading Hester Storm's
Shadows From The Wu-T'ung Tree*

I climb a hill
to keep a tryst with the moon.
Old cultures
struggle to their feet to walk with me
on such a venture.
There's no profit in it.
Just an ancient wind
curling through me
and leaving me with the feeling
i've eaten what Gods eat.